Chapter 1: Embracing Self-Love and Confidence

Recognizing Your Worth

In the busy and often chaotic world we live in, it can be easy to forget our true worth and value. Society is constantly bombarded with messages telling us we need to be more, do more, have more to be successful and happy. But the truth is, you are already enough just as you are. Recognizing your worth is the first step towards embracing your inner strength and cultivating self-love and confidence.

Each day, take a moment to remind yourself of your worth. You are unique and special, with talents and qualities that make you who you are. Embrace your individuality and celebrate the things that make you stand out from the crowd. You have so much to offer the world, and it is important to recognize and appreciate your own value.

Self-love and confidence go hand in hand with recognizing your worth. When you genuinely believe in yourself and your abilities, you exude a sense of confidence that is magnetic and inspiring. Trust in your own worth and know that you deserve all the good things that come your way. Repeat affirmations such as "I am worthy of love and success" or "I believe in my own worth and value" to reinforce these positive beliefs in your mind.

Success and achievement are within your reach when you recognize and embrace your worth. By acknowledging your own value, you empower yourself to pursue your goals and dreams with confidence and determination. Remember that you can achieve remarkable things, and that your worth is not determined by external measures of success. Trust in yourself and your abilities and watch as you accomplish amazing things.

In moments of self-doubt or insecurity, remind yourself of your worth and the incredible potential that lies within you. You can achieve anything you set your mind to, and you deserve all the love, happiness, and success that life has to offer. Embrace your worth and let it guide you on your journey towards self-love, confidence, and fulfillment. You are enough, just as you are.

Cultivating Self-Compassion

Cultivating self-compassion is a crucial aspect of developing a powerful sense of self-love and confidence. It involves treating yourself with kindness, understanding, and forgiveness, just as you would treat a close friend or loved one. By practicing self-compassion, you can learn to be more accepting of your flaws and imperfections and embrace your inner strength.

Each day, take a moment to remind yourself of your worth and value. Repeat affirmations such as "I am deserving of love and respect" or "I am enough just as I am". These positive statements can help rewire your brain to focus on self-love and confidence, rather than self-doubt and criticism. Remember, you are worthy of love and kindness, both from others and from yourself.

When faced with challenges or setbacks, practice self-compassion by acknowledging your feelings and giving yourself permission to experience them fully. Avoid self-criticism and instead, offer yourself words of comfort and understanding. Treat yourself with the same compassion and empathy that you would offer to a friend in need. By cultivating self-compassion in times of difficulty, you can build resilience and inner strength.

Incorporate self-care practices into your daily routine to nurture your mind, body, and spirit. Engage in activities that bring you joy and relaxation, such as meditation, yoga, or spending time in nature. Prioritize your well-being and be available for self-care activities that replenish your energy and nourish your soul. By taking care of yourself, you are showing yourself the love and compassion you deserve.

Remember, self-compassion is a journey, not a destination. Be patient with yourself as you cultivate this important quality. Celebrate your progress and growth, no matter how small. By practicing self-compassion daily, you can strengthen your sense of self-love and confidence, and embrace your inner strength with grace and compassion. You deserve love, kindness, and self-compassion.

Building Confidence in Yourself

Building confidence in yourself is a journey that requires patience, practice, and self-love. It is essential to believe in your abilities and strengths, even when faced with challenges or setbacks. By embracing your inner strength and acknowledging your worth, you can cultivate a sense of confidence that will empower you to achieve your goals and dreams.

One powerful way to boost your confidence is through daily affirmations. By repeating positive statements about yourself and your capabilities, you can rewire your brain to focus on your strengths rather than your weaknesses. Affirmations such as "I am confident in my abilities" or "I believe in myself and my potential" can help you build a solid foundation of self-assurance and resilience.

Another key aspect of building confidence is setting achievable goals and taking small steps towards accomplishing them. By breaking down your goals into manageable tasks, you can build momentum and celebrate your progress along the way. Each small success will reinforce your belief in yourself and your ability to overcome challenges.

Surrounding yourself with supportive and encouraging people can also help boost your confidence. Seek out friends, family members, or mentors who believe in you and your potential. Their positive energy and encouragement can serve as a source of inspiration and motivation as you work towards building your self-confidence.

Remember, building confidence in yourself is a lifelong journey. Embrace your inner strength, practice self-love and acceptance, and believe in your ability to achieve greatness. By cultivating a sense of confidence and self-assurance, you can overcome any obstacles that come your way and live a life filled with purpose, passion, and fulfillment.

Embracing Imperfections

Embracing imperfections is a crucial step in the journey towards self-love and confidence. It is important to remember that no one is perfect, and that it is our flaws and shortcomings that make us unique and beautiful. By accepting and embracing our imperfections, we can learn to love ourselves fully and unconditionally.

Every day, remind yourself that it is okay to be imperfect. Instead of focusing on what you perceive as flaws, try to see them as opportunities for growth and self-improvement. Embrace your imperfections as part of what makes you who you are and remember that they are not a reflection of your worth or value as a person.

When you learn to embrace your imperfections, you will find that you are more confident and self-assured. Instead of constantly striving for perfection, you will be able to appreciate yourself for who you are, flaws and all. This newfound self-acceptance will radiate outwards, allowing you to exude confidence in all areas of your life.

Embracing imperfections also opens the door to creativity and inspiration. When you let go of the need to be perfect, you free yourself from self-imposed limitations and allow yourself to take risks and explore innovative ideas. Embrace your imperfections as opportunities to think creatively and push the boundaries of your creativity.

In conclusion, embracing imperfections is a powerful act of self-love and confidence. By accepting and celebrating your flaws, you will find that you are able to love yourself more fully and authentically. Remember that imperfection is beautiful, and that it is what makes you unique and special. Embrace your imperfections and watch as your self-love and confidence soar to new heights.

Setting Boundaries for Self-Care

Setting boundaries for self-care is an essential practice that allows you to prioritize your well-being and cultivate a sense of inner strength. By establishing boundaries, you are actively choosing to honor your needs and protect your energy from external influences that may drain you. It is important to remember that setting boundaries is not a selfish act, but rather a necessary step towards self-love and confidence.

When setting boundaries for self-care, it is important to first identify what areas of your life may be causing you stress or overwhelm. Take a moment to reflect on your daily routines, relationships, and commitments, and pinpoint where you may be feeling stretched too thin. Once you have identified these areas, you can begin to establish boundaries that will help you maintain a sense of balance and peace.

One way to set boundaries for self-care is to communicate your needs openly and honestly with others. Letting people know what you are comfortable with and what you need to feel supported is key to creating healthy relationships and maintaining your own well-being. Remember, it is okay to say no to things that do not serve you or align with your values - your needs are just as important as anyone else's.

Another important aspect of setting boundaries for self-care is learning to prioritize your own needs and desires. It is easy to focus on the needs of others or societal expectations, but it is crucial to remember that taking care of yourself is not a luxury, but a necessity. By setting boundaries that prioritize your own well-being, you are empowering yourself to live a more fulfilling and authentic life.

In conclusion, setting boundaries for self-care is a powerful act of self-love and confidence that can lead to greater happiness and fulfillment. Remember that you deserve to prioritize your own well-being and set boundaries that support your growth and development. By establishing healthy boundaries, you are allowing yourself to thrive and embrace your inner strength with grace and compassion.

Chapter 2: Daily Affirmations for Self-Love and Confidence

I am worthy of love and respect.

In this subchapter, "I am worthy of love and respect," we will explore the importance of recognizing our own value and deservingness of love and respect. As individuals, we often struggle with self-doubt and feelings of inadequacy, but it is crucial to affirm to ourselves that we are deserving of love and respect in all aspects of our lives.

Each day, take a moment to remind yourself that you are worthy of love and respect. Repeat affirmations such as "I am deserving of love and respect," "I am worthy of all the good things life has to offer," and "I value myself and treat myself with kindness and respect." By affirming these beliefs, you are reinforcing positive self-perception and building a durable foundation of self-love and confidence.

When we believe in our own worthiness, we attract love and respect from others. By radiating self-assurance and self-respect outward, we set the standard for how we should be treated by those around us. Remember that you are a unique and valuable individual, deserving of love, respect, and kindness from others. Embrace your inner strength and let it shine through in all your interactions.

In moments of doubt or insecurity, remind yourself of your inherent worthiness. Reflect on your strengths, accomplishments, and positive qualities, and acknowledge that you are deserving of love and respect simply because you are you. By recognizing and affirming your own value, you set the stage for greater self-love, confidence, and personal growth.

As you continue your journey of self-love and confidence, remember that you are worthy of love and respect in all areas of your life. Embrace your inner strength, believe in your worthiness, and treat yourself with the love and respect you deserve. By affirming these beliefs daily, you will cultivate a deep sense of self-worth and attract positive relationships and opportunities that reflect your true value. You are worthy of love and respect, and it is time to embrace that truth with open arms.

I embrace my uniqueness and individuality.

In this subchapter, we focus on embracing our uniqueness and individuality. It is important to remember that we are all different and that is what makes us special. Embracing our individuality allows us to shine in our own unique way and stand out from the crowd. It is a beautiful thing to celebrate what makes us different and to fully embrace who we are.

Each one of us is unique in our own way, with our own set of strengths, weaknesses, and quirks. Embracing our uniqueness means accepting ourselves for who we are, flaws and all. It means acknowledging our differences and recognizing that they are what make us special. By embracing our individuality, we can fully love and appreciate ourselves for the amazing individuals that we are.

When we embrace our uniqueness, we become more confident in ourselves and our abilities. We no longer feel the need to conform to societal norms or compare ourselves to others. Instead, we stand tall in our individuality and shine brightly for the world to see. By embracing our uniqueness, we can tap into our inner strength and unlock our full potential.

Embracing our individuality also opens a world of possibilities for personal growth and development. When we fully accept ourselves for who we are, we grow and evolve into the best versions of ourselves. By embracing our uniqueness, we can explore new opportunities, take risks, and push ourselves outside of our comfort zones. Our individuality is the key to unlocking our true potential and achieving our goals.

So, let us all embrace our uniqueness and individuality with open arms. Let us celebrate what makes us different and stand tall in our own unique light. By fully accepting and loving ourselves for who we are, we can unlock our inner strength, achieve success, and continue the journey of personal growth and development. Embrace your uniqueness and watch as your confidence soars, your creativity flourishes, and your inner strength shines through.

I trust in my abilities to overcome challenges.

In this subchapter, we remind ourselves of the incredible inner strength that lies within each of us. It is important to affirm to ourselves daily that we have the power and resilience to face any obstacles that come our way. By trusting in our abilities, we can navigate through challenges with confidence and grace.

Each day brings new challenges and opportunities for growth. By affirming our belief in ourselves and our abilities, we can approach these challenges with a positive mindset. We must remember that we can overcome anything that stands in our way.

Trusting in our abilities allows us to tap into our inner strength and face challenges head-on.

When we face challenges with a mindset of trust in our abilities, we open ourselves up to new possibilities and opportunities for growth and success. By affirming our belief in ourselves, we can conquer even the most daunting obstacles. Trusting in our abilities empowers us to take risks, try new things, and achieve our goals.

As we affirm our trust in our abilities to overcome challenges, we also cultivate self-love and confidence. By believing in ourselves, we are showing ourselves the love and respect we deserve. This self-love and confidence radiate from within us, empowering us to face challenges with courage and determination.

In conclusion, trust in your abilities to overcome challenges is a powerful affirmation that can guide you on your journey to self-love, confidence, success, and personal growth. By embracing this affirmation, you are acknowledging your inner strength and resilience. Remember, you can overcome any challenge that comes your way. Trust in yourself, believe in your abilities, and watch as you conquer obstacles with grace and ease.

I deserve happiness and fulfillment.

In this subchapter, 'I am deserving of happiness and fulfillment,' we will explore the power of self-love and confidence in achieving true fulfillment in life. It is important to remember that you are worthy of happiness and fulfillment, no matter what challenges you may face. By embracing your inner strength and believing in your own worth, you can manifest the life you truly desire.

Each day, take a moment to affirm to yourself, 'I am deserving of happiness and fulfillment.' Repeat this affirmation with conviction and belief, allowing it to sink into your subconscious mind. By affirming your worthiness, you are setting the intention to attract positivity and abundance into your life.

Remember that self-love and confidence are essential components of success and achievement. When you believe in yourself and your abilities, you are more likely to take risks and pursue your dreams. By affirming your worthiness of happiness and fulfillment, you are paving the way for greater success and achievement in all areas of your life.

As you continue to affirm your worthiness of happiness and fulfillment, you will notice a shift in your mindset and outlook on life. You will begin to attract more positive experiences and opportunities, as you radiate self-love and confidence from within. Trust in the power of affirmations to transform your life and bring you closer to the happiness and fulfillment you deserve.

In conclusion, remember that you ARE deserving of happiness and fulfillment. Embrace your inner strength, cultivate self-love and confidence, and believe in your own worth. By affirming your worthiness each day, you are opening yourself up to a world of possibilities and abundance. Trust in yourself and your ability to create the life you truly desire.

I radiate positivity and self-assurance.

In this subchapter, we focus on the power of radiating positivity and self-assurance in our daily lives. It is important to remember that the energy we put out into the world is reflected back to us, so by exuding confidence and positivity, we attract the same energy in return. When we believe in ourselves and our abilities, we open ourselves up to endless possibilities and opportunities for growth and success.

Each day, take a moment to affirm to yourself, ... Repeat this affirmation throughout the day, especially in moments of doubt or insecurity. By reminding yourself of your inner strength and worth, you will begin to see a shift in your mindset and attitude towards yourself and others.

When we radiate positivity and self-assurance, we not only uplift ourselves but also inspire those around us. Our confidence and self-assurance can be contagious, spreading a wave of empowerment and encouragement to those we interact with. By becoming a beacon of light and positivity, we can create a ripple effect of confidence and self-love in our communities and relationships.

Remember that self-love and confidence are not selfish acts but essential components of personal growth and development. By embracing and nurturing these qualities within us, we become better equipped to manage life's challenges and setbacks with grace and resilience. Trust in your abilities and believe in your worth, knowing that you can achieve remarkable things.

As you go about your day, embody the affirmation, "I radiate positivity and self-assurance," in all that you do. By choosing to focus on the positive aspects of yourself and your life, you invite more abundance and joy into your experience. Embrace your inner strength and shine brightly with confidence and self-love, knowing that you are deserving of all the success and happiness that comes your way.

Chapter 3: Daily Affirmations for Success and Achievement

I am capable of achieving my goals.

In this subchapter, I want to remind you that you are truly capable of achieving your goals. No matter how big or small they may seem, with determination and hard work, you can make them a reality. Believe in yourself and your abilities and know that you have the inner strength to overcome any obstacles that may come your way.

Each day, affirm to yourself that you can achieve your goals. Repeat positive affirmations such as "I am strong, capable, and determined" or "I have the power within me to reach my full potential." By focusing on these affirmations daily, you will begin to shift your mindset and believe in your own abilities more deeply.

Remember that success and achievement are not defined by the opinions of others, but by your own personal growth and development. Set realistic and attainable goals for yourself and celebrate each small victory along the way. By acknowledging your progress and staying focused on your end goal, you will build the confidence and self-love needed to keep pushing forward.

Creativity and inspiration are key components to achieving your goals. Allow yourself to think creatively and explore new ways to approach challenges.

Embrace your creative side and let it guide you towards innovative solutions and fresh ideas. Surround yourself with inspiration, whether it be through art, music, or nature, to keep your motivation levels high.

In conclusion, always remember that you can achieve your goals. Believe in yourself, stay focused, and never give up on your dreams. With self-love, confidence, and a positive mindset, you can conquer any obstacles that stand in your way. Embrace your inner strength and watch as you soar to new heights of success and achievement.

I attract abundance and prosperity into my life.

Every day, I affirm to myself that I am deserving of all the good things that come my way. By focusing on positivity and gratitude, I can attract more abundance into my life. The universe wants me to succeed and thrive, and I am open to receiving all the blessings that are meant for me.

As I repeat this affirmation daily, I am strengthening my belief in my own worthiness and ability to manifest my desires. I am confident in my ability to create the life I want, filled with prosperity and abundance. By setting positive intentions and taking inspired action, I am aligning myself with the energy of abundance and attracting more opportunities for success into my life.

I am grateful for all the abundance that surrounds me, both big and small. I appreciate the abundance of love, joy, and opportunities that come my way. I know that by focusing on gratitude and abundance, I am inviting even more blessings into my life. I trust that the universe will always provide for me and support me on my journey towards success and fulfillment.

I release any limiting beliefs or fears that may be holding me back from fully embracing abundance and prosperity. I choose to let go of any scarcity mindset and instead embrace a mindset of abundance and possibility. I am open to receiving all the abundance that is meant for me, and I am excited to see what blessings will come my way.

I am a magnet for abundance and prosperity. I am confident in my ability to attract all the good things that I desire into my life. I am grateful for the abundance that surrounds me, I trust that the universe will always provide for me. I am open to receiving all the blessings that are meant for me, and I am excited to see how my life will continue to unfold with abundance and prosperity.

I am persistent and determined in my pursuits.

In the journey towards self-love and confidence, it is essential to cultivate persistence and determination in our pursuits. It is through these qualities that we can overcome obstacles and challenges that may come our way. By affirming to ourselves that we are persistent and determined, we are setting the stage for success and achievement in all areas of our lives.

Each day, remind yourself of your strength and resilience. Repeat to yourself, "I am persistent and determined in my pursuits." By affirming this statement, you are reinforcing your belief in your abilities and capabilities. You are affirming that you have what it takes to overcome any obstacles that stand in your way.

Persistence and determination are key ingredients for personal growth and development. By staying committed to your goals and dreams, you are taking steps towards becoming the best version of yourself. Remember, it is not about how fast you reach your destination, but rather about the journey and the lessons you learn along the way.

In moments of doubt or uncertainty, lean on your affirmations for strength and guidance. Remind yourself that you can achieve anything you set your mind to. Trust in your abilities and believe in yourself. With persistence and determination, you can accomplish wonderful things and reach new heights of success and achievement.

Embrace your inner strength and harness the power of persistence and determination. By affirming your belief in yourself each day, you are laying the foundation for a life filled with self-love, confidence, and personal growth. Trust in yourself, believe in your abilities, and never give up on your dreams. You can achieve anything you set your mind to, and you have the strength and determination to make it happen.

I celebrate my achievements, big and small.

In this subchapter, we will explore the importance of celebrating our achievements, no matter how big or small. It is crucial to acknowledge and appreciate the progress we make every day, as it helps boost our self-love and confidence. By recognizing our accomplishments, we can cultivate a positive mindset and continue to strive for success.

Each day, take a moment to reflect on your achievements, no matter how minor they may seem. Whether you completed a challenging task at work or simply got out of bed on time, every accomplishment deserves recognition. By celebrating these moments, you are affirming your worth and capabilities, which will in turn fuel your self-love and confidence.

Remember, your success is not measured by grand gestures or major milestones. It is often the small victories that pave the way for greater achievements. By acknowledging and celebrating even the tiniest wins, you are setting yourself up for continued success and growth. Embrace each accomplishment with gratitude and pride, knowing that you are one step closer to reaching your goals.

As you continue to celebrate your achievements, you will begin to see a shift in your mindset. You will start to believe in your abilities and see your worth more clearly. This newfound confidence will empower you to take on new challenges and pursue your dreams with unwavering determination. By celebrating your achievements, you are cultivating a keen sense of self-love and confidence that will carry you through any obstacles that come your way.

So, take the time each day to celebrate your achievements, big and small. Embrace your inner strength and acknowledge the progress you have made. By doing so, you will build a foundation of self-love and confidence that will propel you towards success and fulfillment in all areas of your life. Celebrate yourself, for you are worthy of all the love and praise in the world.

I believe in my potential to create a successful future.

In this subchapter, 'I believe in my potential to create a successful future,' we will explore the power of self-belief and confidence in achieving your goals and dreams. It is important to acknowledge your own potential and trust in your abilities to create the future you desire. By affirming your belief in yourself, you are setting the stage for success and growth in all areas of your life.

Each day, take a moment to remind yourself of your potential and the endless possibilities that lie ahead. By focusing on your strengths and abilities, you are paving the way for a successful future filled with abundance and fulfillment. Trust in yourself and your capabilities and watch as opportunities unfold before you.

As you continue to affirm your belief in your potential, you will notice a shift in your mindset and attitude towards life. You will begin to approach challenges with confidence and determination, knowing that you have what it takes to overcome any obstacles that come your way. Your self-belief will serve as a guiding light, leading you towards a future filled with success and achievement.

Remember, you can create the life you desire. By believing in your potential and trusting in your abilities, you are taking the first step towards a successful future. Embrace your inner strength and confidence and watch as your dreams become a reality. You have the power within you to achieve greatness - believe in yourself and the possibilities are endless.

In conclusion, affirm your belief in your potential each day and watch as your confidence grows, and your future unfolds before you. Trust in yourself and your abilities and know that you are destined for success. Embrace your inner strength and confidence and create the future you desire. Your potential is limitless - believe in yourself and the world is yours to conquer.

Chapter 4: Daily Affirmations for Personal Growth and Development

I am open to new opportunities for growth.

In this subchapter, we explore the power of embracing change and welcoming new experiences into our lives. It is essential to remain open-minded and receptive to the endless possibilities that come our way. By staying open to new opportunities, we allow ourselves to grow and evolve in ways we never thought possible.

Each day presents us with a chance to learn, to expand our horizons, and to challenge ourselves to become the best version of who we are. By affirming our willingness to embrace new opportunities for growth, we set ourselves on a path towards self-discovery and personal development. It is through these experiences that we truly begin to understand our inner strength and potential.

By affirming our openness to growth, we invite success and achievement into our lives. We create space for new ideas, new skills, and new perspectives to flourish. By taking risks and stepping outside of our comfort zones, we allow ourselves to reach new heights and accomplish our goals. Embracing change is essential for personal growth and development, and by affirming our readiness for new opportunities, we set ourselves up for success.

Creativity and inspiration are fueled by our willingness to explore new avenues and try new things. By remaining open to new opportunities for growth, we invite creativity to flow freely and inspire us to think creatively. It is through these moments of exploration and discovery that we uncover hidden talents and passions within ourselves. By affirming our receptiveness to growth, we give ourselves permission to tap into our creative potential and express ourselves in unique and meaningful ways.

In conclusion, by affirming our openness to new opportunities for growth, we set the stage for a journey of self-love and confidence. We empower ourselves to embrace change, welcome success, cultivate personal growth, and unleash our creativity. Each day is a new chance to affirm our readiness for growth and to explore the endless possibilities that lie ahead. Let us continue to affirm our openness to new opportunities and watch as our lives transform in incredible ways.

I embrace challenges as opportunities to learn and grow.

In the journey of self-love and confidence, it is important to embrace challenges as opportunities to gain experience and grow. Challenges are not obstacles, but rather steppingstones on the path to personal growth and development. By shifting our mindset and viewing challenges as opportunities for growth, we can cultivate a sense of resilience and inner strength that will carry us through any adversity.

Each challenge we face is an opportunity to learn something new about ourselves and the world around us. Instead of shying away from challenges, we should welcome them with open arms, knowing that each challenge is an opportunity for personal growth and development. Embracing challenges allows us to push past our comfort zones and discover our true potential.

When we embrace challenges as opportunities to gain experience and grow, we can cultivate a sense of self-love and confidence that is unshakeable. By facing challenges head-on, we can prove to ourselves that we can overcome any obstacle that comes our way. This sense of accomplishment and self-assurance is essential for building a solid foundation of self-love and confidence.

As we navigate through life, challenges will inevitably arise. Instead of viewing challenges as setbacks, we should view them as opportunities for success and achievement. By embracing challenges with a positive mindset, we can pave the way for personal growth and development that will lead us to success and achievement in all areas of our lives.

In conclusion, embracing challenges as opportunities to gain experience and grow is essential for cultivating self-love, confidence, and personal growth. By shifting our mindset and viewing challenges as steppingstones on the path to success, we can unlock our true potential and achieve greatness in all areas of our lives. Embrace challenges with courage and determination, knowing that each challenge is an opportunity for growth and self-discovery.

I prioritize self-improvement and personal development.

In this subchapter, we will explore the importance of prioritizing self-improvement and personal development in our daily lives. It is essential to be available for self-care and growth, as it allows us to become the best versions of ourselves. By focusing on our own well-being and personal growth, we can cultivate a sense of inner strength and confidence that will propel us towards our goals and dreams.

Each day, take a moment to reflect on your personal growth journey and celebrate the progress you have made. Whether it is learning a new skill, overcoming a fear, or simply taking time for self-care, every step towards self-improvement is a victory worth acknowledging. By acknowledging and celebrating your achievements, you are reinforcing positive behaviors and building your self-confidence.

Remember that self-improvement is a lifelong journey, and it is okay to take small steps towards your goals. Set realistic and achievable milestones for yourself and celebrate each milestone as a steppingstone towards your ultimate vision of success. By breaking down your goals into manageable tasks, you can build momentum and stay motivated on your personal development journey.

Surround yourself with positive influences and seek out resources that support your personal growth and development. Whether it is reading self-help books, attending workshops, or seeking guidance from a mentor, there are endless opportunities for learning and growth. Embrace new challenges and opportunities for growth, and always strive to become the best version of yourself.

By prioritizing self-improvement and personal development, you are investing in your own well-being and future success. Embrace the journey of self-discovery and growth and remember that you can achieve great things. Believe in yourself, celebrate your achievements, and continue to strive for personal growth and development every day.

I trust in my ability to adapt to change.

In this subchapter, "I trust in my ability to adapt to change," we explore the power of resilience and flexibility in the face of life's inevitable twists and turns. Change can be intimidating, but by affirming our belief in our own adaptability, we can approach new challenges with confidence and grace.

As we repeat this affirmation daily, we remind ourselves that change is not something to fear, but rather an opportunity for growth and transformation. We trust in our ability to navigate uncertain times with strength and resilience, knowing that we can adapt to whatever life throws our way.

When we trust in our ability to adapt to change, we open ourselves up to new possibilities and opportunities. Instead of resisting change, we embrace it as a chance to learn and evolve. By affirming our confidence in our adaptability, we invite positive energy and abundance into our lives.

This affirmation is especially powerful for those seeking self-love and confidence, success and achievement, personal growth and development, creativity, and inspiration. By trusting in our ability to adapt to change, we can overcome obstacles, reach our goals, and tap into our inner strength and creativity.

So let us repeat this affirmation daily, with a sense of empowerment and optimism. Let us trust in our ability to adapt to change, knowing that we are resilient, flexible, and capable of overcoming any challenge that comes our way. Embrace change with confidence and grace and watch as your life transforms in beautiful and unexpected ways.

I am constantly evolving and becoming the best version of myself.

In this subchapter, we explore the powerful concept of constantly evolving and becoming the best version of ourselves. It is a journey of self-discovery and growth that requires dedication, perseverance, and a deep commitment to self-love and confidence. As we embrace our inner strength, we unlock our true potential and unleash our creativity and inspiration.

Each day presents a new opportunity to gain experience, grow, and evolve. By setting daily affirmations for self-love and confidence, we can cultivate a positive mindset and empower ourselves to overcome challenges and achieve success. Affirmations serve as powerful reminders of our worth and capabilities, helping us to stay focused on our goals and dreams.

As we commit to personal growth and development, we open ourselves up to endless possibilities and opportunities for transformation. It is through this process that we discover our true passions and purpose and unleash our creativity and inspiration. By embracing our inner strength, we can break free from self-limiting beliefs and step into our full potential.

Remember, growth is a continuous process that requires patience and self-compassion. It is important to celebrate our progress and achievements, no matter how small, and to acknowledge the effort and dedication we put into becoming the best version of ourselves. By practicing daily affirmations for success and achievement, we can stay motivated and inspired to keep moving forward on our journey of self-discovery.

So, embrace the journey of self-evolution with an open heart and a positive mindset. Trust in your inner strength and believe in your ability to become the best version of yourself. With daily affirmations for self-love and confidence, success and achievement, personal growth and development, and creativity and inspiration, you can unlock your true potential and create a life filled with love, joy, and abundance.

Chapter 5: Daily Affirmations for Creativity and Inspiration

I am a vessel for creativity and innovation.

In this subchapter, we explore the powerful affirmation: "I am a vessel for creativity and innovation." As we journey through life, it is important to remind ourselves that we can tap into our inner creativity and use it to drive innovation in all aspects of our lives. By embracing this affirmation, we open ourselves up to endless possibilities and opportunities for growth and success.

Each day, as we repeat this affirmation to ourselves, we are reinforcing the belief that we can think creatively, to see solutions where others see obstacles, and to bring innovative ideas and perspectives to the table. This affirmation serves as a reminder that we aren't limited by our circumstances or past experiences, but rather empowered by our own creative potential.

When we fully embrace the idea that we are vessels for creativity and innovation, we can approach challenges with a sense of curiosity and excitement, rather than fear or doubt. We become more willing to take risks, try new things, and push ourselves beyond our comfort zones. This mindset shift can lead to breakthroughs in our personal and professional lives, allowing us to achieve levels of success and achievement that we may have never thought possible.

By incorporating this affirmation into our daily routine, we are nurturing a sense of self-love and confidence that is essential for personal growth and development. We are acknowledging our own worth and abilities and recognizing that we have the power to create positive change in our lives and the world around us. This affirmation serves as a constant reminder that we are capable of greatness, and that our creativity and innovation are valuable assets that should be embraced and celebrated.

So, let us affirm to ourselves each day: 'I am a vessel for creativity and innovation.' Let us believe in our own potential to bring current ideas and solutions to the table, and to make a positive impact on the world. By embracing our inner strength and creativity, we can unlock new levels of success, achievement, and personal growth that will enrich our lives and inspire those around us.

I trust in my creative instincts and ideas.

In this subchapter, we explore the power of believing in ourselves and our unique abilities to create. Trusting in our creative instincts is essential for nurturing our inner strength and confidence. When we listen to our intuition and follow our ideas, we unlock a world of possibilities and opportunities for growth and success.

It is important to remember that our creative instincts are a gift that sets us apart from others. Each of us has a unique perspective and vision that can inspire and uplift those around us. By trusting in our creative instincts, we allow ourselves to fully express who we are and share our talents with the world. Embracing our creativity is a powerful way to cultivate self-love and confidence.

As we affirm our trust in our creative instincts and ideas, we pave the way for success and achievement. When we believe in ourselves and our abilities, we attract positive energy and opportunities that align with our goals and dreams. By staying true to our creative vision and following our intuition, we can manifest our deepest desires and aspirations. Trusting in our creative instincts is the key to unlocking our full potential and achieving our highest aspirations.

Our creative instincts are a source of personal growth and development. When we trust in our ideas and allow ourselves to explore new possibilities, we expand our horizons and push past our comfort zones. Embracing our creativity opens doors to new experiences and challenges that help us evolve and grow as individuals. By trusting in our creative instincts, we invite personal growth and development into our lives, leading to a deeper sense of self-awareness and fulfillment.

In conclusion, trusting in our creative instincts and ideas is a powerful affirmation of self-love and confidence. By believing in ourselves and our unique abilities, we open ourselves up to a world of creativity, inspiration, and success. Embracing our creative instincts allows us to express our true selves and share our gifts with the world. Let us affirm our trust in our creative instincts and ideas, knowing that they are the key to unlocking our inner strength and achieving our highest potential.

I find inspiration in everyday moments and experiences.

In our fast-paced world, it is easy to overlook the beauty and inspiration that surrounds us in our everyday lives. From the laughter of a loved one to the colors of a sunset, there are countless moments and experiences that can lift our spirits and ignite our creativity. By taking the time to pause and appreciate these simple joys, we can find renewed strength and confidence within ourselves.

Each day is filled with opportunities to find inspiration, whether it is in the smile of a stranger or the sound of birds chirping outside your window. By opening your heart and mind to the world around you, you can tap into a wellspring of creativity and motivation that will propel you towards your goals. Embrace each moment as a gift, and let it fuel your journey towards self-love and confidence.

It's important to remember that inspiration can come from the most unexpected places. A chance encounter, a fleeting thought, or a mundane task can spark a wave of creativity and innovation within you. By remaining open and receptive to these everyday moments, you can cultivate a sense of wonder and excitement that will drive you towards success and achievement.

Take the time each day to reflect on the moments that bring you joy and inspiration. Whether it is a quiet moment of reflection or a burst of energy from a new idea, honor these experiences and allow them to guide you towards personal growth and development. Embrace the beauty of the present moment and watch as your confidence and self-love blossom in its wake.

As you journey through life, remember that inspiration is all around you, waiting for you to discover it in the smallest of moments. By cultivating a mindset of gratitude and openness, you can tap into an endless well of creativity and inspiration that will empower you to achieve your dreams. Embrace the magic of everyday moments and let them fill you with the strength and confidence you need to shine brightly in the world.

I allow myself to think creatively and explore new possibilities.

In this subchapter, we are going to explore the power of thinking creatively and opening ourselves up to new possibilities. It is important to remember that growth and self-love come from stepping outside our comfort zones and embracing the unknown. By allowing ourselves to think creatively and explore innovative ideas, we open ourselves up to endless opportunities for personal growth and success.

Each day, we have the choice to break free from the limitations we place on ourselves and start thinking in a new way. By challenging our beliefs and stepping outside of our comfort zones, we can uncover hidden talents and passions that we never knew existed. Embracing the unknown can be scary, but it is also incredibly rewarding. When we allow ourselves to be creative, we give ourselves the chance to discover new paths and opportunities that we may have never considered before.

By affirming to ourselves that we are open to new possibilities and willing to explore different ideas, we are setting ourselves up for success and personal growth. It is important to remember that there is no right or wrong way to think, and by allowing ourselves to think creatively, we are giving ourselves permission to dream big and reach for the stars. By embracing this mindset, we can tap into our inner strength and confidence, leading us to new levels of success and achievement.

As we continue our journey of self-love and confidence, it is important to remind ourselves that thinking creatively is a powerful tool for personal growth and development. By breaking free from limiting beliefs and exploring new possibilities, we can unlock our full potential and create a life filled with purpose and passion. By embracing creativity and inspiration, we can tap into our unique talents and gifts, leading us to a life that is truly fulfilling and meaningful.

So, I encourage you to take a moment each day to affirm to yourself that you are open to new possibilities and willing to think freely. By doing so, you are giving yourself permission to explore innovative ideas and embrace the unknown. Remember, the possibilities are endless when we allow ourselves to think creatively and step outside of our comfort zones. Embrace the power of being creative and watch as your life unfolds in ways you never thought possible.

I am a source of inspiration and creativity for myself and others.

In this subchapter, we will explore the power of being a source of inspiration and creativity for ourselves and others. It is important to recognize the impact we have on those around us, and the positive energy we can bring into their lives. By embracing our inner strength and sharing our creativity with the world, we can inspire others to do the same.

Each day, take a moment to reflect on the ways in which you inspire yourself and those around you. Whether it be through your words, actions, or creative endeavors, remember that you have the power to uplift and motivate others. By acknowledging your own strengths and talents, you can cultivate a sense of self-love and confidence that will radiate outwards.

As you continue your journey of self-discovery and personal growth, remember that you are a beacon of light for others. Your unique perspective and creative spirit can help to ignite the flames of inspiration in those around you. By sharing your gifts with the world, you are not only enriching your own life but also bringing joy and positivity to those who cross your path.

It is important to nurture your creativity and embrace your inner strength each day. By setting aside time for self-care and reflection, you can tap into your creative potential and inspire others to do the same. Whether it be through writing, painting, music, or any other form of expression, allow yourself to explore your creativity and share it with the world.

Start your day by affirming, "I am deserving of love and respect." Remember that you are worthy of all the good things life has to offer. By recognizing your own value, you open yourself up to receiving the love and respect you deserve from others. Embrace this affirmation wholeheartedly and watch as it transforms your relationships and interactions with those around you.

Affirm to yourself, "I am confident in my abilities and decisions." Trust in yourself and your intuition. Believe that you have the knowledge and skills necessary to succeed in any endeavor you choose to pursue. By affirming your confidence, you will find the courage to take risks, make bold decisions, and step outside of your comfort zone to achieve your goals.

Repeat to yourself, "I am constantly growing and evolving." Embrace change and challenge yourself to step out of your comfort zone. Personal growth comes from pushing yourself beyond your limits and exploring new opportunities for self-improvement. Embrace this affirmation as a reminder that growth is a natural part of life, and that every experience, whether positive or negative, has the potential to shape you into a stronger, more resilient individual.

Affirm, "I am a creative being with limitless potential." Tap into your imagination and embrace your unique creativity. Allow yourself to explore current ideas, experiment with different mediums, and express yourself freely. By affirming your creativity, you open yourself up to new possibilities and opportunities for inspiration. Believe in your ability to create and innovate and watch as your creative energy flows effortlessly into every aspect of your life!

Affirmations

Below are listings of affirmations for each day for one year, grouped by week. Space is included for you to record the thoughts and feelings brought forth by the affirmations. Embrace these daily affirmations to cultivate self-love, confidence, success, personal growth, and creativity in your life. You can achieve greatness by embracing your inner strength.

Each day, take a moment to remind yourself of your worth and potential. Repeat these affirmations with conviction and belief and watch as they manifest in your life. Incorporate these daily affirmations into your routine and watch as they empower you to cultivate self-love, confidence, success, personal growth, and creativity in your life. You can achieve greatness and embrace your inner strength. Believe in yourself, trust in your abilities, and never underestimate the power of positive affirmations to shape your reality. Embrace these affirmations with an open heart and a positive mindset and watch as they transform your life in ways you never thought possible.

Week One:

Day 1: I am worthy of love and respect.

Day 2: I believe in myself and my abilities.

Day 3: I deserve to be happy and successful.

Day 4: I am confident in who I am and what I can achieve.

Day 5: I am grateful for the person I am becoming.

Day 6: I can overcome any challenges that come my way.

Day 7: I radiate positivity and kindness.

_____

_____

_____

_____

_____

_____

_____

Week Two:

Day 8: I am enough just as I am.

Day 9: I embrace my fears and transform them into strengths.

Day 10: I trust in my intuition and inner wisdom.

Day 11: I am surrounded with love and support.

Day 12: I am resilient and can bounce back from any setbacks.

Day 13: I am open to new opportunities and experiences.

Day 14: I am a magnet for miracles and blessings.

_____

_____

_____

_____

_____

_____

_____

Week Three:

Day 15: I choose to see the good in myself and others.

Day 16: I am the architect of my life; I build its foundation and choose its contents.

Day 17: I am at peace with who I am and where I am going.

Day 18: I release all negative thoughts and embrace positivity.

Day 19: I am a work in progress, and that is okay.

Day 20: I am learning and growing every day.

Day 21: I am deserving of all the good things life has to offer.

_____

_____

_____

_____

_____

_____

_____

Week Four:

Day 22: I am confident in my decisions and choices.

Day 23: I am brave, bold, and beautiful.

Day 24: I am worthy of all the success coming my way.

Day 25: I am a beacon of light and love to those around me.

Day 26: I radiate confidence and self-assurance.

Day 27: I am in control of my thoughts and emotions.

Day 28: I am a powerhouse of positivity and optimism.

_____

_____

_____

_____

_____

_____

_____

Week Five:

Day 29: I am surrounded by abundance and prosperity.

Day 30: I trust the process of life and know that everything is unfolding as it should.

Day 31: I am a unique and special individual.

Day 32: I am grateful for all the love in my life.

Day 33: I forgive myself for past mistakes and release them with love.

Day 34: I am worthy of all the good things that come my way.

Day 35: I am powerful enough to create the life of my dreams.

_____

_____

_____

_____

_____

_____

_____

Week Six:

Day 36: I am a vessel of love and light.

Day 37: I am open to giving and receiving love freely.

Day 38: I am confident in my abilities and talents.

Day 39: I am deserving of all the good things life has to offer.

Day 40: I am a strong, capable, and resilient person.

Day 41: Love, joy, and abundance surround me.

Day 42: I believe in my unlimited potential.

_____

_____

_____

_____

_____

_____

_____

Week Seven:

Day 43: I am a magnet for positive energy and opportunities.

Day 44: I am a source of inspiration to others.

Day 45: I am grateful for the abundance in my life.

Day 46: I trust in the divine plan for my life.

Day 47: I am worthy of all the success and happiness in the world.

Day 48: I am a powerful creator of my reality.

Day 49: Love, joy, and peace fulfill me.

_____

_____

_____

_____

_____

_____

Week Eight:

Day 50: I am a unique and valuable person.

Day 51: I am confident in my ability to achieve my goals.

Day 52: I am open to receiving all the blessings the universe has in store for me.

Day 53: I deserve love and respect from others.

Day 54: I trust in my own inner guidance.

Day 55: I can achieve anything I set my mind to.

Day 56: I am a masterpiece in progress.

_____

_____

_____

_____

_____

_____

_____

Week Nine:

Day 57: I am a beacon of light and love to those around me.

Day 58: I am a magnet for success and prosperity.

Day 59: I am worthy of all the good things life has to offer.

Day 60: I am fearless in the pursuit of my dreams.

Day 61: Love, joy, and clarity surround me.

Day 62: I am grateful for the beauty and wonder of life.

Day 63: I am confident in my ability to overcome any obstacles.

_____

_____

_____

_____

_____

_____

_____

Week Ten:

Day 64: I am a radiant being of light and love.

Day 65: I am open to new opportunities and experiences.

Day 66: I am deserving of all the good things that come my way.

Day 67: I trust in the timing of my life and know that everything happens for a reason.

Day 68: I am a powerful creator of my reality.

Day 69: I am worthy of all the love and happiness the universe has to offer. I radiate confidence, strength, and positivity in everything I do.

Day 70: I am grateful for my unique gifts and talents.

_____

_____

_____

_____

_____

_____

_____

Week Eleven:

Day 71: I am a magnet for positive energy and opportunities.

Day 72: I am worthy of love, joy, and abundance.

Day 73: I believe in the power of my dreams and aspirations.

Day 74: I am resilient and can overcome any challenges that come my way.

Day 75: I am open to receiving all the blessings the universe has in store for me.

Day 76: I trust in the journey of my life and know that everything is unfolding as it should.

Day 77: I am fearless in the pursuit of my goals and passions.

_____

_____

_____

_____

_____

_____

_____

Week Twelve:

Day 78: I am deserving of all the success and happiness in the world.

Day 79: I radiate confidence, strength, and positivity.

Day 80: I am a vessel of love and light, spreading kindness wherever I go.

Day 81: I am grateful for the abundance of blessings in my life.

Day 82: I trust in the wisdom of my heart and intuition.

Day 83: I am worthy of all the love and respect in the world.

Day 84: I am a beacon of inspiration and motivation to others.

_____

_____

_____

_____

_____

_____

_____

Week Thirteen:

Day 85: I can achieve greatness in all areas of my life.

Day 86: I am open to the infinite possibilities that the universe has in store for me.

Day 87: I am deserving of all the good things that come my way.

Day 88: I trust in the divine timing of my life's path.

Day 89: I am a powerful creator of my reality, shaping it with love and positivity.

Day 90: A supportive and loving community surrounds me.

Day 91: I am a masterpiece in progress, constantly evolving and growing.

_____

_____

_____

_____

_____

_____

Week Fourteen:

92. I am worthy of love and respect from myself and others. I treat myself with kindness and compassion.

93. I trust in my journey and know that challenges are opportunities for growth and learning. I face obstacles with courage and resilience.

94. I am a magnet for positivity and abundance. I attract all good things into my life with ease and gratitude.

95. I embrace my uniqueness and celebrate my individuality. I am confident in who I am and what I have to offer.

96. I forgive myself for past mistakes and release all self-judgment. I deserve forgiveness, love, and happiness.

97. I am a powerhouse of creativity and inspiration. I express myself authentically and share my gifts with the world.

98. I choose to focus on the present moment and appreciate the beauty and blessings that surround me. I am at peace with where I am right now.

_____

_____

_____

_____

_____

Week Fifteen:

Day 99: I am a source of light and inspiration to those around me.

Day 100: I believe in my unlimited potential and the infinite possibilities of my future.

Day 101: I am confident in my decisions and trust in my inner wisdom.

Day 102: I am deserving of love, happiness, and fulfillment in all areas of my life.

Day 103: I am a warrior of light, shining brightly in the darkness.

Day 104: I am open to new adventures, growth, and transformation.

Day 105: I am grateful for the abundance of love and joy that surrounds me.

_____

_____

_____

_____

_____

_____

_____

Week Sixteen:

Day 106: I trust in the journey of my soul and embrace all that it brings.

Day 107: I am a powerful force of love and positivity, creating a ripple effect of goodness.

Day 108: I am worthy of all the success, prosperity, and happiness that life has to offer.

Day 109: I believe in my abilities and know that I can achieve anything I set my mind to.

Day 110: I am a magnet for miracles and blessings, attracting positivity and abundance into my life.

Day 111: I am grateful for the challenges that have made me stronger and more resilient.

Day 112: I trust in the process of growth and change, knowing that it leads to greater heights.

_____

_____

_____

_____

_____

_____

_____

Week Seventeen:

Day 113: I am deserving of all the good things that come my way, embracing them with an open heart.

Day 114: I am a beacon of light and love, illuminating the path for others to follow.

Day 115: I am confident in my abilities, talents, and gifts, using them to create a better world.

Day 116: I am open to receiving love, kindness, and support from others.

Day 117: I trust in the universe's plan for me, surrendering to its guidance and wisdom.

Day 118: I am worthy of all the love, joy, and abundance that life has to offer.

Day 119: I believe in my dreams and aspirations, knowing that they are within reach.

_____

_____

_____

_____

_____

_____

_____

Week Eighteen:

Day 120: I am a warrior of light, spreading positivity, hope, and compassion wherever I go.

Day 121: I am grateful for the beauty and wonder of life, finding joy in the little things.

Day 122: I trust in my intuition and inner knowing, following its guidance with confidence.

Day 123: I am deserving of all the success, happiness, and fulfillment that I desire.

Day 124: I trust in my abilities and believe in my potential to achieve remarkable things. I am capable, resilient, and unstoppable.

Day 125: Love, light, and positive energy surround me. I allow it to uplift and inspire me.

Day 126: I am open to the abundance of the universe, receiving its gifts with gratitude and joy.

_____

_____

_____

_____

_____

_____

Week Nineteen:

Day 127: I trust in the timing of my life's journey, knowing that every experience serves a purpose.

Day 128: I am worthy of all the blessings and opportunities that come my way, embracing them with an open heart.

Day 129: I believe in my inner strength and resilience, knowing that I can overcome any challenge.

Day 130: I am a beacon of hope and encouragement to those in need, offering support and compassion.

Day 131: I am grateful for the lessons and growth that come from facing adversity with courage and grace.

Day 132: I trust in the power of self-love and acceptance, recognizing my worth and value as a unique individual.

Day 133: I am deserving of all the love, happiness, and success that I seek, allowing them to flow into my life effortlessly.

_____

_____

_____

_____

_____

_____

_____

Week Twenty:

Day 134: I am a vessel of peace and harmony, spreading tranquility and serenity wherever I go.

Day 135: I am open to the infinite possibilities that the universe has in store for me, welcoming new experiences, and adventures.

Day 136: I trust in the wisdom of the universe, surrendering to its guidance and direction with faith and trust.

Day 137: I am a magnet for positive relationships and connections, attracting kindred spirits and supportive allies.

Day 138: I am grateful for the abundance of creativity and inspiration that flows through me, fueling my passion and purpose.

Day 139: I believe in the power of forgiveness and letting go, freeing myself from past hurts and resentments.

Day 140: I am worthy of all the blessings and miracles that come my way, receiving them with grace and gratitude.

_____

_____

_____

_____

_____

Week Twenty-One:

Day 141: I am a force of nature, embodying strength, resilience, and determination in the face of challenges.

Day 142: I am open to the transformative power of love, allowing it to heal and nurture my heart and soul.

Day 143: I trust in the process of growth and evolution, embracing change as a catalyst for personal development and renewal.

Day 144: I am deserving of all the joy, abundance, and fulfillment that life has to offer, accepting them with an open heart.

Day 145: I am a radiant being of light and love, shining brightly in the darkness and illuminating the path for others.

Day 146: I am confident in my abilities and talents, using them to create a life of purpose, passion, and meaning.

Day 147: A supportive and loving community envelope me, nurturing relationships that bring out the best in me.

_____

_____

_____

_____

Week Twenty-Two:

Day 148: I am a masterpiece in progress, evolving and growing with each new experience and opportunity.

Day 149: I am a magnet for success, prosperity, and abundance, attracting wealth and opportunity into my life.

Day 150: I am grateful for the lessons and challenges that have shaped me into the resilient and compassionate person I am today.

Day 151: I trust in the divine timing of my life's path, knowing that everything happens for a reason and serves my highest good.

Day 152: I am a powerful creator of my reality, manifesting my dreams and desires with clarity, intention, and purpose.

Day 153: I am worthy of all the love, joy, and peace that life has to offer, embracing them with an open heart and grateful spirit.

Day 154: I believe in the power of positivity and optimism, cultivating a mindset of abundance and possibility.

_____

_____

_____

Week Twenty-Three:

Day 155: I am confident in my abilities and talents, trusting in my unique gifts and strengths to guide me towards success and fulfillment.

Day 156: I am open to the flow of life, surrendering to the natural rhythm and cycles of growth, change, and transformation.

Day 157: I am deserving of all the blessings and miracles that come my way, receiving them with gratitude, humility, and joy.

Day 158: I trust in the wisdom of the universe, surrendering to its divine guidance and direction with faith, trust, and surrender.

Day 159: I am a magnet for positive energy and opportunities, attracting abundance, prosperity, and success into my life effortlessly.

Day 160: I am grateful for the beauty and wonder of life, finding joy, peace, and inspiration in the simple pleasures and moments of each day.

Day 161: I believe in my unlimited potential and the infinite possibilities that lie ahead, embracing the future with hope, courage, and determination.

_____

_____

_____

_____

Week Twenty-Four:

Day 162: I am confident in my decisions and choices, knowing that they are guided by my intuition, wisdom, and inner knowing.

Day 163: I am open to receiving love, kindness, and support from others, allowing their generosity and compassion to nurture and uplift me.

Day 164 Affirmation: I am the architect of my life, and I build its foundation with love, strength, and positivity. I embrace challenges as opportunities for growth and transformation.

Day 165: I am a beacon of light and positivity, spreading love, kindness, and compassion wherever I go.

Day 166: I am a magnet for miracles and blessings, attracting abundance, joy, and prosperity into my life.

Day 167: I am grateful for the challenges that have shaped me into the strong, resilient, and empathetic person I am today.

Day 168: I trust in the divine timing of my life's path, knowing that every experience, setback, and success serves a greater purpose.

_____

_____

_____

_____

Week Twenty-Five:

Day 169: I am a powerful creator of my reality, shaping my thoughts, words, and actions to manifest my dreams and desires.

Day 170: I am worthy of all the love, joy, and peace that life has to offer, embracing them with an open heart and grateful spirit.

Day 171: I believe in the power of positivity and optimism, cultivating a mindset of abundance, possibility, and growth.

Day 172: I am confident in my abilities and talents, trusting in my unique gifts and strengths to guide me towards success and fulfillment.

Day 173: I am open to the flow of life, surrendering to the natural rhythm and cycles of growth, change, and transformation.

Day 174: I am deserving of all the blessings and miracles that come my way, receiving them with gratitude, humility, and joy.

Day 175: I trust in the wisdom of the universe, surrendering to its divine guidance and direction with faith, trust, and surrender.

_____

_____

_____

Week Twenty-Six:

Day 176: I am a magnet for positive energy and opportunities, attracting abundance, prosperity, and success into my life effortlessly.

Day 177: I am grateful for the beauty and wonder of life, finding joy, peace, and inspiration in the simple pleasures and moments of each day.

Day 178: I believe in my unlimited potential and the infinite possibilities that lie ahead, embracing the future with hope, courage, and determination.

Day 179: I am confident in my decisions and choices, knowing they are guided by my intuition, wisdom, and inner knowing.

Day 180: I am open to receiving love, kindness, and support from others, allowing their generosity and compassion to nurture and uplift me.

Day 181: I trust in the goodness of humanity, believing in the power of connection, empathy, and understanding to create positive change in the world.

Day 182: I am a vessel of peace and harmony, radiating tranquility, compassion, and love to all beings and the world around me.

_____

_____

_____

Week Twenty-Seven:

Day 183: I am worthy of all the success, happiness, and fulfillment that life has to offer, embracing them with an open heart and a spirit of gratitude.

Day 184: I believe in the power of self-love and acceptance, recognizing my worth, value, and beauty as a unique and precious soul.

Day 185: I am a beacon of light and hope, shining brightly in the darkness and illuminating the path for others to follow.

Day 186: I am a force of nature, embodying strength, resilience, and courage in the face of challenges, setbacks, and obstacles.

Day 187: I am open to the transformative power of love, allowing it to heal, nourish, and uplift my heart, mind, and spirit.

Day 188: I trust in the process of growth and evolution, embracing change, transformation, and renewal as opportunities for personal development and self-discovery.

Day 189: I am deserving of all the joy, abundance, and fulfillment that life has to offer, accepting them with an open heart and a spirit of gratitude.

_____

_____

_____

Week Twenty-Eight:

Day 190: I am a radiant being of light and love, spreading positivity, kindness, and compassion wherever I go.

Day 191: I am confident in my abilities and talents, using them to create a life of purpose, passion, and meaning for myself and others.

Day 192: I am surrounded by a supportive and loving community, nurturing relationships that bring out the best in me and support my growth.

Day 193: I am a masterpiece in progress, evolving, growing, and expanding with each new experience, challenge, and opportunity that comes my way.

Day 194: I am a magnet for success, prosperity, and abundance, attracting wealth, opportunity, and fulfillment into my life with ease and grace.

Day 195: I am grateful for the lessons and challenges that have shaped me into the resilient, compassionate, and empathetic person I am today.

Day 196: I trust in the divine timing of my life's path, knowing that everything unfolds in perfect alignment with my soul's growth, evolution, and purpose.

_____

_____

_____

Week Twenty-Nine:

Day 197: I am a powerful creator of my reality, manifesting my dreams, desires, and intentions with clarity, focus, and positive energy.

Day 198: I am worthy of all the blessings, miracles, and wonders that come my way, receiving them with an open heart, a spirit of gratitude, and a sense of awe.

Day 199: I believe in the magic of new beginnings, fresh starts, and endless possibilities that each day brings.

Day 200: I am a living expression of love, compassion, and kindness, radiating warmth and positivity to those around me.

Day 201: I am a magnet for abundance in all its forms - wealth, health, love, and happiness flow effortlessly into my life.

Day 202: I trust in the journey of self-discovery and personal growth, embracing every experience as an opportunity to gain experience, learn and evolve.

Day 203: I am worthy of all the blessings and opportunities that come my way, accepting them with grace and gratitude.

_____

_____

_____

Week Thirty:

Day 204: I am a beacon of light in times of darkness, offering hope, encouragement, and support to those in need.

Day 205: I believe in the power of my dreams, aspirations, and desires, knowing that they are within reach and achievable.

Day 206: I am confident in my ability to overcome challenges, setbacks, and obstacles with resilience, determination, and grace.

Day 207: I am open to the wisdom of the universe, surrendering to its guidance and direction with faith, trust, and surrender.

Day 208: I am deserving of all the love, joy, and peace that life has to offer, embracing them with an open heart and a spirit of gratitude.

Day 209: I am a powerhouse of positivity, optimism, and enthusiasm, spreading joy, light, and inspiration wherever I go.

Day 210: I am grateful for the beauty, wonder, and magic that surrounds me, finding joy and peace in the present moment.

_____

_____

_____

Week Thirty-One:

Day 211: I trust in the process of growth, change, and transformation, knowing that every experience serves a purpose and leads to greater heights.

Day 212: I am worthy of all the success, happiness, and fulfillment that life has to offer, accepting them with an open heart and a spirit of gratitude.

Day 213: I believe in the power of self-love, self-acceptance, and self-compassion, recognizing my worth, value, and uniqueness as a divine being.

Day 214: I am a beacon of light and hope, shining brightly in the darkness and illuminating the path for others to follow.

Day 215: I am a force of nature, embodying strength, resilience, and courage in the face of challenges, setbacks, and obstacles.

Day 216: I am open to the transformative power of love, allowing it to heal, nourish, and uplift my heart, mind, and spirit.

Day 217: I trust in the process of growth and evolution, embracing change, transformation, and renewal as opportunities for personal development and self-discovery.

_____

_____

Week Thirty-Two:

Day 218: I am deserving of all the joy, abundance, and fulfillment that life has to offer, accepting them with an open heart and a spirit of gratitude.

Day 219: I am a radiant being of light and love, spreading positivity, kindness, and compassion wherever I go.

Day 220: I am confident in my abilities and talents, using them to create a life of purpose, passion, and meaning for myself and others.

Day 221: A supportive and loving community surrounds me; nurturing relationships that bring out the best in me and support my growth.

Day 222: I am a masterpiece in progress, evolving, growing, and expanding with each new experience, challenge, and opportunity that comes my way.

Day 223: I am a magnet for success, prosperity, and abundance, attracting wealth, opportunity, and fulfillment into my life with ease and grace.

Day 224: I am grateful for the lessons and challenges that have shaped me into the resilient, compassionate, and empathetic person I am today.

_____

_____

_____

Week Thirty-Three:

Day 225: I trust in the divine timing of my life's path, knowing that everything unfolds in perfect alignment with my soul's growth, evolution, and purpose.

Day 226: I am a powerful creator of my reality, manifesting my dreams, desires, and intentions with clarity, focus, and positive energy.

Day 227: I am worthy of all the blessings, miracles, and wonders that come my way, receiving them with an open heart, a spirit of gratitude, and a sense of awe.

Day 228: I believe in the power of intention, visualization, and manifestation, aligning my thoughts, beliefs, and actions with my deepest desires and dreams.

Day 229: I am a magnet for positive energy, opportunities, and experiences, attracting abundance, success, and joy into my life effortlessly.

Day 230: I am grateful for the abundance, beauty, and wonder of the world around me, finding peace, joy, and inspiration in nature and the present moment.

Day 231: I trust in the process of growth, change, and transformation, knowing that every experience, challenge, and opportunity leads to greater awareness and evolution.

Week Thirty-Four:

Day 232: I am deserving of all the good things that come into my life. I release all self-doubt and embrace my worthiness with open arms.

Day 233: I embrace the journey of self-discovery and personal growth, recognizing that each step forward brings me closer to my true self.

Day 234: I am a beacon of light and positivity, illuminating the path for myself and others with love, compassion, and empathy.

Day 235: I trust in the abundance of the universe, knowing that there is always enough love, joy, and prosperity to go around.

Day 236: I believe in my inner strength and resilience, understanding that I have the power to overcome any challenge that comes my way.

Day 237: I am open to the flow of life, allowing experiences, emotions, and opportunities to come and go with ease and grace.

Day 238: I am deserving of all the blessings and miracles that the universe has in store for me, accepting them with gratitude and humility.

_____

_____

_____

Week Thirty-Five:

Day 239: I am a source of inspiration and empowerment to those around me, encouraging them to embrace their own unique gifts and talents.

Day 240: I am grateful for the beauty and wonder of the world, finding joy and peace in the simple moments and connections that bring me happiness.

Day 241: I trust in the path that is unfolding before me, knowing that every twist and turn is leading me towards my highest good.

Day 242: I am worthy of all the success, love, and abundance that life has to offer, welcoming these gifts with an open heart and mind.

Day 243: I believe in the power of self-love and acceptance, recognizing my true worth and value as a divine being of light.

Day 244: I am a force of nature, embodying resilience, courage, and determination in the face of challenges and obstacles.

Day 245: I am open to the transformative power of love, allowing it to heal and nourish my heart, mind, and spirit.

_____

_____

_____

Week Thirty-Six:

Day 246: I trust in the process of growth and evolution, embracing change, transformation, and renewal as opportunities for personal development and self-discovery.

Day 247: I am deserving of all the joy, abundance, and fulfillment that life has to offer, accepting them with an open heart and a spirit of gratitude.

Day 248: I am a radiant being of light and love, spreading positivity, kindness, and compassion wherever I go.

Day 249: I am confident in my abilities and talents, using them to create a life of purpose, passion, and meaning for myself and others.

Day 250: I am surrounded by a supportive and loving community, nurturing relationships that bring out the best in me and support my growth.

Day 251: I am a masterpiece in progress, evolving, growing, and expanding with each new experience, challenge, and opportunity that comes my way.

Day 252: I am a magnet for success, prosperity, and abundance, attracting wealth, opportunity, and fulfillment into my life with ease and grace.

_____

_____

_____

Week Thirty-Seven:

Day 253: I am grateful for the lessons and challenges that have shaped me into the resilient, compassionate, and empathetic person I am today.

Day 254: I trust in the divine timing of my life's path, knowing that everything unfolds in perfect alignment with my soul's growth, evolution, and purpose.

Day 255: I am a powerful creator of my reality, manifesting my dreams, desires, and intentions with clarity, focus, and positive energy.

Day 256: I am worthy of all the blessings, miracles, and wonders that come my way, receiving them with an open heart, a spirit of gratitude, and a sense of awe.

Day 257: I believe in the power of intention, visualization, and manifestation, aligning my thoughts, beliefs, and actions with my deepest desires and dreams.

Day 258: I am a magnet for positive energy, opportunities, and experiences, attracting abundance, success, and joy into my life effortlessly.

Day 259: I am grateful for the abundance, beauty, and wonder of the world around me, finding peace, joy, and inspiration in nature and the present moment.

_____

_____

Week Thirty-Eight:

Day 260: I trust in the process of growth, change, and transformation, knowing that every experience, challenge, and opportunity leads to greater awareness and evolution.

Day 261: I am worthy of all the love, respect, and admiration that I receive from others, acknowledging my own worth and value as a unique individual.

Day 262: I believe in the power of self-expression, creativity, and authenticity, allowing my true self to shine brightly in all that I do.

Day 263: I am open to the wisdom of the universe, surrendering to its guidance, support, and protection with faith, trust, and surrender.

Day 264: I am deserving of all the love, joy, and abundance that life has to offer, embracing them with an open heart and a spirit of gratitude.

Day 265: I am a beacon of light and hope, shining brightly in the darkness and illuminating the path for others to follow.

Day 266: I trust in the divine timing of my life, knowing that everything unfolds in perfect harmony for my highest good and growth.

_____

_____

_____

Week Thirty-Nine:

Day 267: I am a vessel of peace and harmony, radiating tranquility and compassion to those around me.

Day 268: I am open to the infinite possibilities that the universe offers, welcoming new adventures and experiences with an open heart.

Day 269: I am deserving of all the blessings that flow into my life, embracing them with gratitude and grace.

Day 270: I believe in the power of resilience and perseverance, knowing that I can overcome any obstacle that stands in my way.

Day 271: I am a beacon of light and inspiration, encouraging others to shine their own unique brilliance.

Day 272: I am grateful for the abundance of love, joy, and support that surrounds me each day.

Day 273: I trust in the process of growth and transformation, embracing change as an opportunity for personal evolution.

_____

_____

_____

_____

_____

Week Forty:

Day 274: I am worthy of all the success, happiness, and fulfillment that I desire, and I attract them effortlessly into my life.

Day 275: I believe in the beauty of my dreams and aspirations, and I have faith that they will manifest in perfect timing.

Day 276: I am a magnet for positive energy and opportunities, attracting abundance and prosperity into my life.

Day 277: I am open to giving and receiving love unconditionally, creating deep and meaningful connections with others.

Day 278: I am grateful for the lessons that challenges bring, as they strengthen me and lead me to greater understanding.

Day 279: I trust in the wisdom of my intuition, knowing that it guides me towards my highest path and purpose.

Day 280: I am deserving of all the blessings and miracles that come my way, and I receive them with an open heart and mind.

_____

_____

_____

Week Forty-One:

Day 281: I am a source of light and love, bringing warmth and compassion to all those I encounter.

Day 282: I am confident in my abilities and talents, and I use them to create positive change in the world.

Day 283: I am surrounded by a supportive community that uplifts and inspires me to be my best self.

Day 284: I am a masterpiece in progress, continually evolving and growing into the fullest expression of myself.

Day 285: I am a magnet for success, attracting opportunities and achievements that align with my highest good.

Day 286: I am grateful for the challenges that have shaped me, as they have made me stronger and more resilient.

Day 287: I trust in the journey of my life, knowing that every experience has a purpose and leads me towards greater fulfillment.

_____

_____

_____

_____

_____

Week Forty-Two:

Day 288: I am a powerful creator of my reality, shaping my thoughts and beliefs to manifest my deepest desires.

Day 289: I am worthy of all the love, joy, and peace that life has to offer, and I welcome them into my heart with gratitude.

Day 290: I believe in the power of self-compassion and forgiveness, releasing any self-judgment with love and understanding.

Day 291: I am open to the guidance of the universe, surrendering to its wisdom and trusting in its divine plan for me.

Day 292: I am deserving of all the good things that come my way, and I accept them with an open heart and mind.

Day 293: I am a beacon of light and hope, shining brightly in times of darkness and inspiring others to do the same.

Day 294: I trust in the process of growth and transformation, knowing that change leads to new opportunities and blessings.

_____

_____

_____

Week Forty-Three:

Day 295: I am worthy of all the love, respect, and admiration that I receive, as I honor and value myself deeply.

Day 296: I believe in the power of authenticity and vulnerability, as they allow me to connect deeply with myself and others.

Day 297: I am open to the wisdom of the universe, knowing that it guides me towards my highest good with love and compassion.

Day 298: I am deserving of all the love, joy, and abundance that life has to offer, and I receive these gifts with an open heart and mind.

Day 299: I am a beacon of light and hope, shining brightly in the darkness and illuminating the path for others to follow.

Day 300: I trust in the divine timing of my life, knowing that everything unfolds in perfect harmony for my highest good and growth.

Day 301: I am a vessel of peace and harmony, radiating tranquility and compassion to those around me.

_____

_____

_____

Week Forty-Four:

Day 302: I am open to the infinite possibilities that the universe offers, welcoming new adventures and experiences with an open heart.

Day 303: I am deserving of all the blessings that flow into my life, embracing them with gratitude and grace.

Day 304: I believe in the power of resilience and perseverance, knowing that I can overcome any obstacle that stands in my way.

Day 305: I radiate confidence, inner peace, and positivity. I trust in the process of life and know that I am exactly where I need to be.

Day 306: I am a beacon of light and love, illuminating the world with positivity, compassion, and kindness.

Day 307: I trust in the journey of self-discovery and growth, knowing that every experience leads me closer to my true self.

Day 308: I am open to receiving abundance in all areas of my life - financially, emotionally, spiritually, and physically.

_____

_____

_____

_____

Week Forty-Five:

Day 309: I believe in my inner strength and resilience, allowing me to face challenges with courage and determination.

Day 310: I am deserving of all the blessings and opportunities that come my way, and I welcome them with an open heart.

Day 311: I am a source of inspiration and motivation to those around me, encouraging them to pursue their dreams and passions.

Day 312: I am grateful for the abundance of love, joy, and support that fills my life each day.

Day 313: I trust in the process of growth and transformation, knowing that change is necessary for personal evolution and progress.

Day 314: I am worthy of all the success, happiness, and fulfillment that I desire, and I attract them effortlessly into my life.

Day 315: I believe in the power of visualization and manifestation, aligning my thoughts and beliefs with my dreams and goals.

_____

_____

_____

_____

Week Forty-Six:

Day 316: I am a magnet for positive energy and opportunities, attracting abundance, prosperity, and success into my life.

Day 317: I am open to giving and receiving love unconditionally, fostering deep and meaningful connections with others.

Day 318: I am grateful for the lessons that challenges bring, as they provide me with growth, strength, and wisdom.

Day 319: I trust in the wisdom of my intuition, following its guidance towards my highest path and purpose.

Day 320: I am deserving of all the blessings and miracles that come my way, and I receive them with gratitude and humility.

Day 321: I am a source of light and love, bringing warmth and compassion to all those I encounter.

Day 322: I am confident in my abilities and talents, using them to create positive change in the world.

_____

_____

_____

_____

Week Forty-Seven:

Day 323: I am surrounded by a supportive community that uplifts and inspires me to be my best self.

Day 324: I am a masterpiece in progress, continually evolving and growing into the fullest expression of myself.

Day 325: I am a magnet for success, attracting opportunities and achievements that align with my highest good.

Day 326: I am grateful for the challenges that have shaped me, as they have made me stronger and more resilient.

Day 327: I trust in the journey of my life, knowing that every experience has a purpose and leads me towards greater fulfillment.

Day 328: I am a powerful creator of my reality, shaping my thoughts and beliefs to manifest my deepest desires.

Day 329: I am worthy of all the love, joy, and peace that life has to offer, and I welcome them into my heart with gratitude.

_____

_____

_____

_____

Week Forty-Eight:

Day 330: I believe in the power of self-compassion and forgiveness, releasing any self-judgment with love and understanding.

Day 331: I am open to the guidance of the universe, surrendering to its wisdom and trusting in its divine plan for me.

Day 332: I am deserving of all the good things that come my way, and I accept them with an open heart and mind.

Day 333: I am a beacon of light and hope, shining brightly in times of darkness and inspiring others to do the same.

Day 334: I trust in the process of growth and transformation, knowing that change leads to new opportunities and blessings.

Day 335: I am worthy of all the love, respect, and admiration that I receive, as I honor and value myself deeply.

Day 336: I believe in the power of authenticity and vulnerability, as they allow me to connect deeply with myself and others.

_____

_____

_____

Week Forty-Nine:

Day 337: I am open to the wisdom of the universe, knowing that it guides me towards my highest good with love and compassion.

Day 338: I am deserving of all the love, joy, and abundance that life has to offer, and I receive these gifts with an open heart and mind.

Day 339: I am a beacon of light and hope, shining brightly in the darkness and illuminating the path for others to follow.

Day 340: I trust in the divine timing of my life, knowing that everything unfolds in perfect harmony for my highest good and growth.

Day 341: I am a vessel of peace and harmony, radiating tranquility and compassion to those around me.

Day 342: I am open to the infinite possibilities that the universe offers, welcoming new adventures and experiences with an open heart.

Day 343: I am deserving of all the blessings that flow into my life, embracing them with gratitude and grace.

_____

_____

_____

_____

Week Fifty:

Day 344: I am a beacon of love, light, and positivity. My heart is open to giving and receiving love, and I attract positive energy into my life.

Day 345: I am grateful for the abundance in my life. I attract prosperity, love, and happiness effortlessly, and I am open to receiving all the blessings that come my way.

Day 346: I trust in the flow of life, allowing experiences to unfold with ease and grace, knowing that everything happens for a reason.

Day 347: I am open to the abundance of the universe, welcoming prosperity, joy, and love into every aspect of my life.

Day 348: I believe in my inner strength and resilience, empowering me to face challenges with courage and determination.

Day 349: I am deserving of all the blessings and opportunities that come my way, embracing them with gratitude and a humble heart.

Day 350: I am a source of inspiration and motivation, encouraging others to embrace their passions and pursue their dreams.

_____

_____

_____

Week Fifty-One:

Day 351: I am grateful for the abundance of love, joy, and support that surrounds me every day, uplifting my spirit and nourishing my soul.

Day 352: I trust in the process of growth and transformation, knowing that change is essential for personal evolution and self-discovery.

Day 353: I am worthy of all the success, happiness, and fulfillment that I desire, and I attract them effortlessly into my life.

Day 354: I believe in the power of visualization and manifestation, aligning my thoughts and beliefs with my dreams and goals.

Day 355: I am a magnet for positive energy and opportunities, attracting abundance, prosperity, and success into every area of my life.

Day 356: I am open to giving and receiving love unconditionally, cultivating deep and meaningful connections with those around me.

Day 357: I am grateful for the lessons that challenges bring, as they provide me with growth, strength, and wisdom.

_____

_____

_____

Week Fifty-Two:

Day 358: I trust in the wisdom of my intuition, following its guidance towards my highest path and purpose with faith and confidence.

Day 359: I am deserving of all the blessings and miracles that come my way, and I receive them with gratitude and a heart full of appreciation.

Day 360: I am a beacon of light and love, spreading warmth, kindness, and compassion wherever I go.

Day 361: I am confident in my abilities and talents, using them to create positive change and have influence in the world.

Day 362: A supportive community that uplifts, surrounds and inspires me to be my best self and reach my highest potential.

Day 363: I am a masterpiece in progress, continually evolving and growing into the fullest expression of my authentic self.

Day 364: I am a magnet for success, attracting opportunities and achievements that align with my purpose and bring me fulfillment.

Day 365: I am grateful for the challenges that have shaped me and the growth they have brought, making me stronger, wiser, and more resilient.

In conclusion, remember that you are a source of inspiration and creativity for yourself and others.

Embrace your inner strength, cultivate self-love and confidence, and share your creative spirit with the world. By doing so, you will not only enrich your own life but also positively impact those around you.

Keep shining brightly and inspiring others on their own journeys of self-love, confidence, success, and creativity!

Made in the USA
Monee, IL
25 November 2024

71242067R00077